We Like

WHORE

Brilliant Swear Word To Color

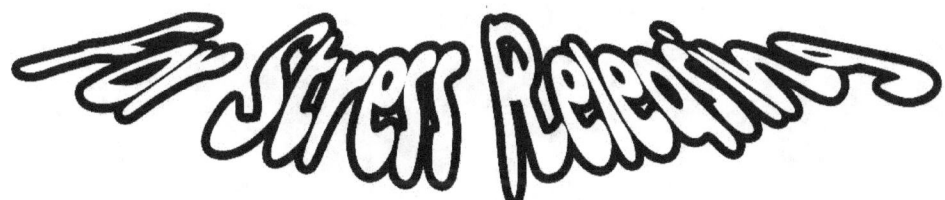

For Stress Releasing

Bear Smith Ebot

Happy Coloring!

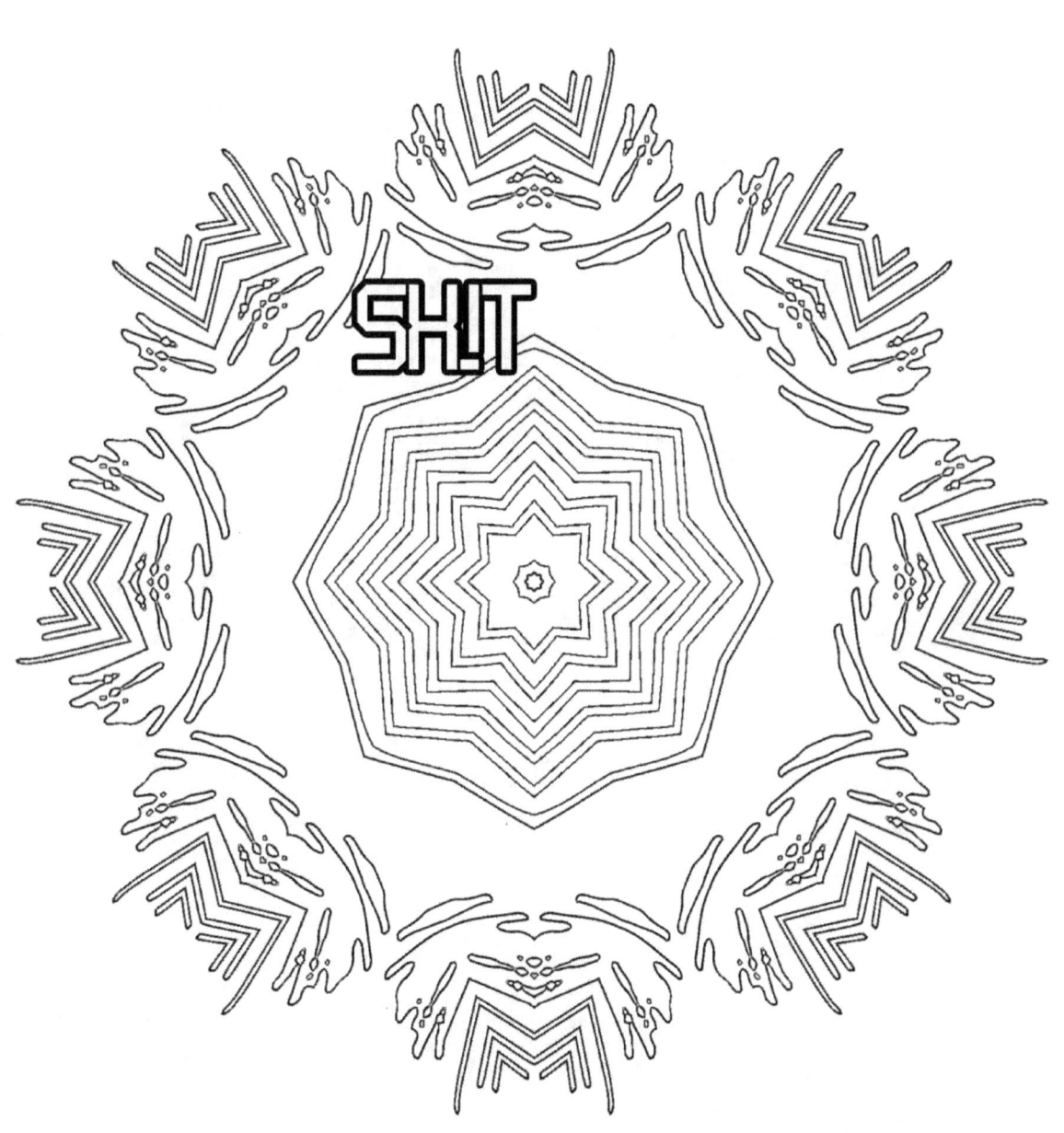

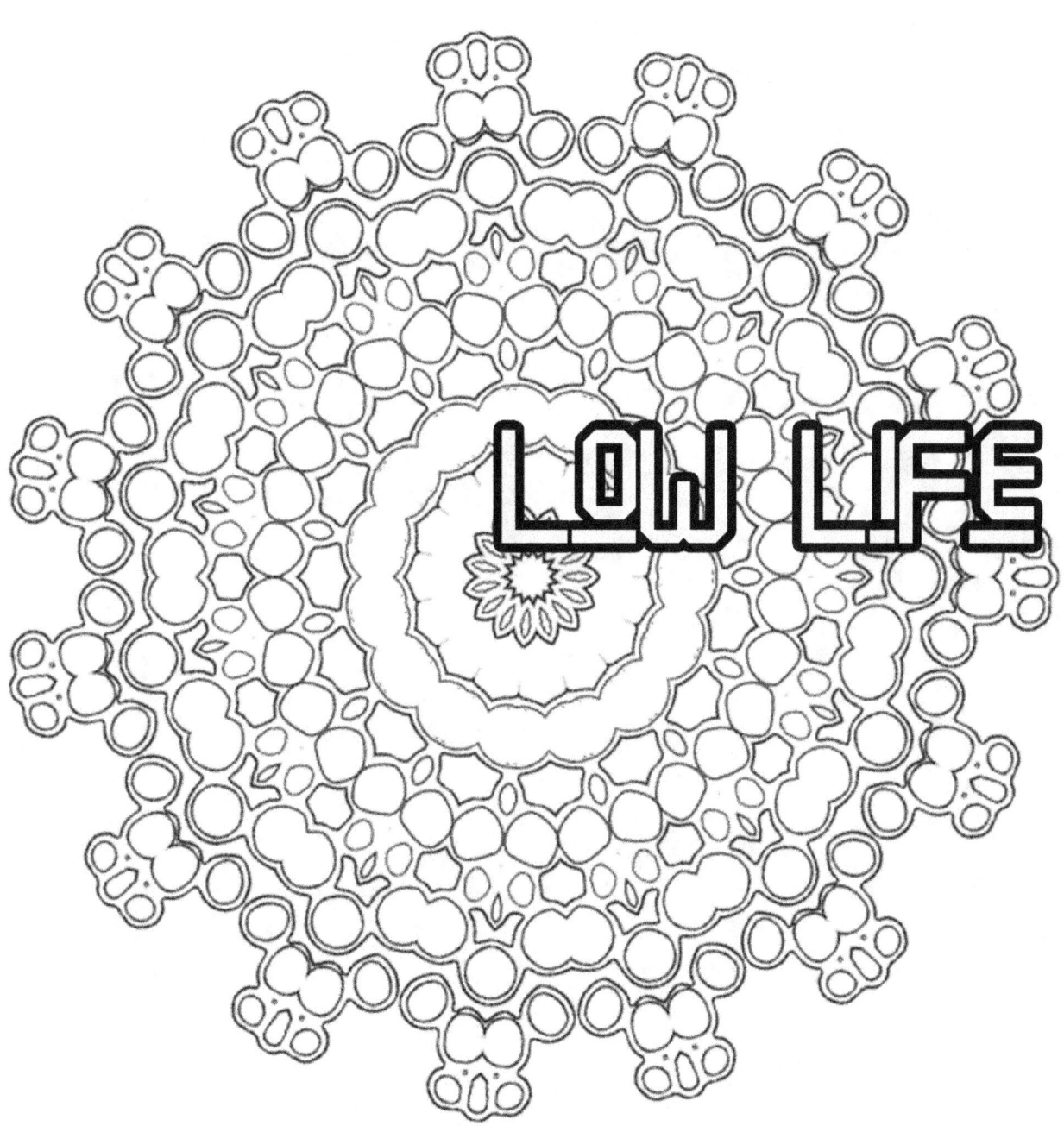

LOW LIFE

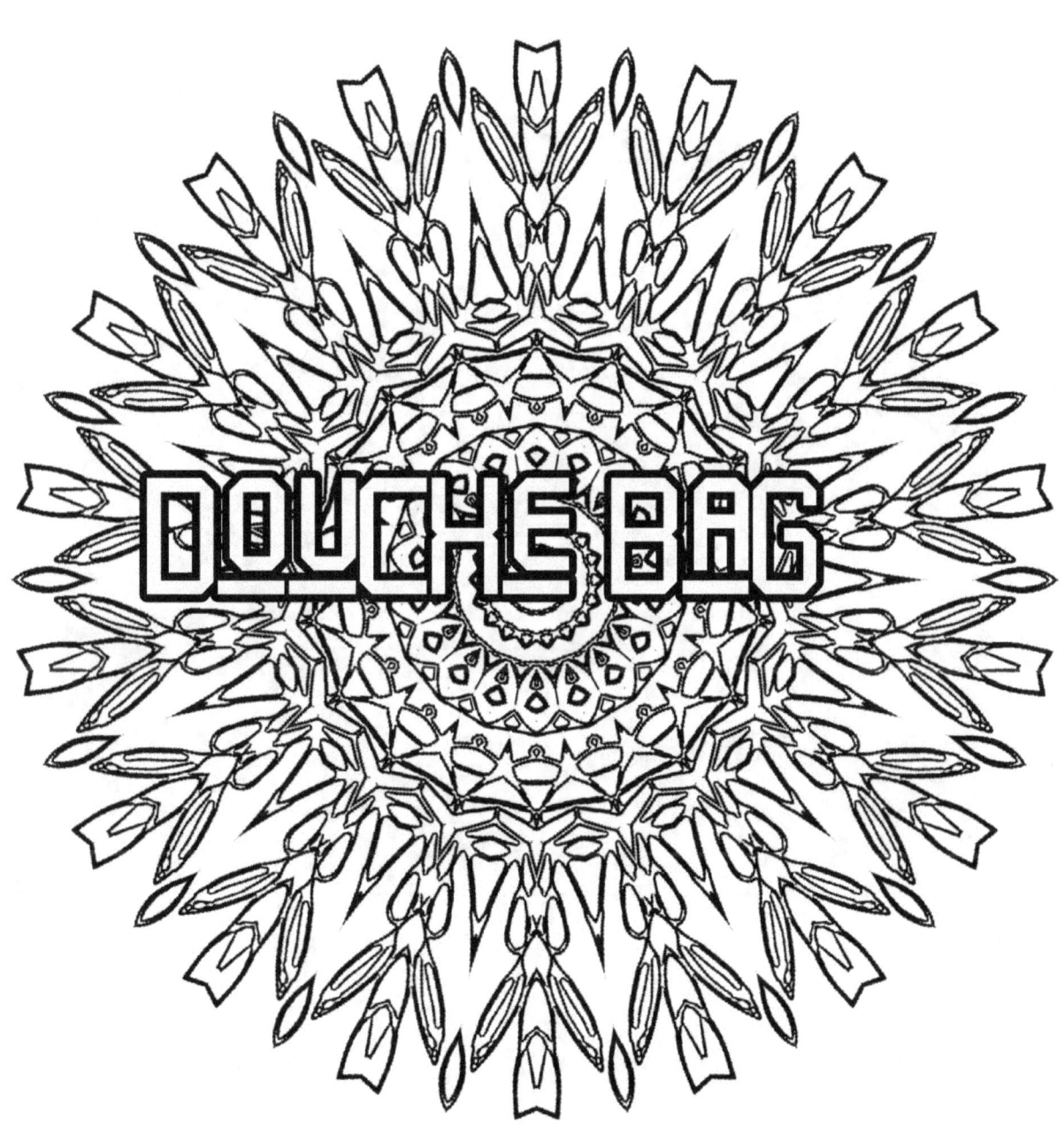

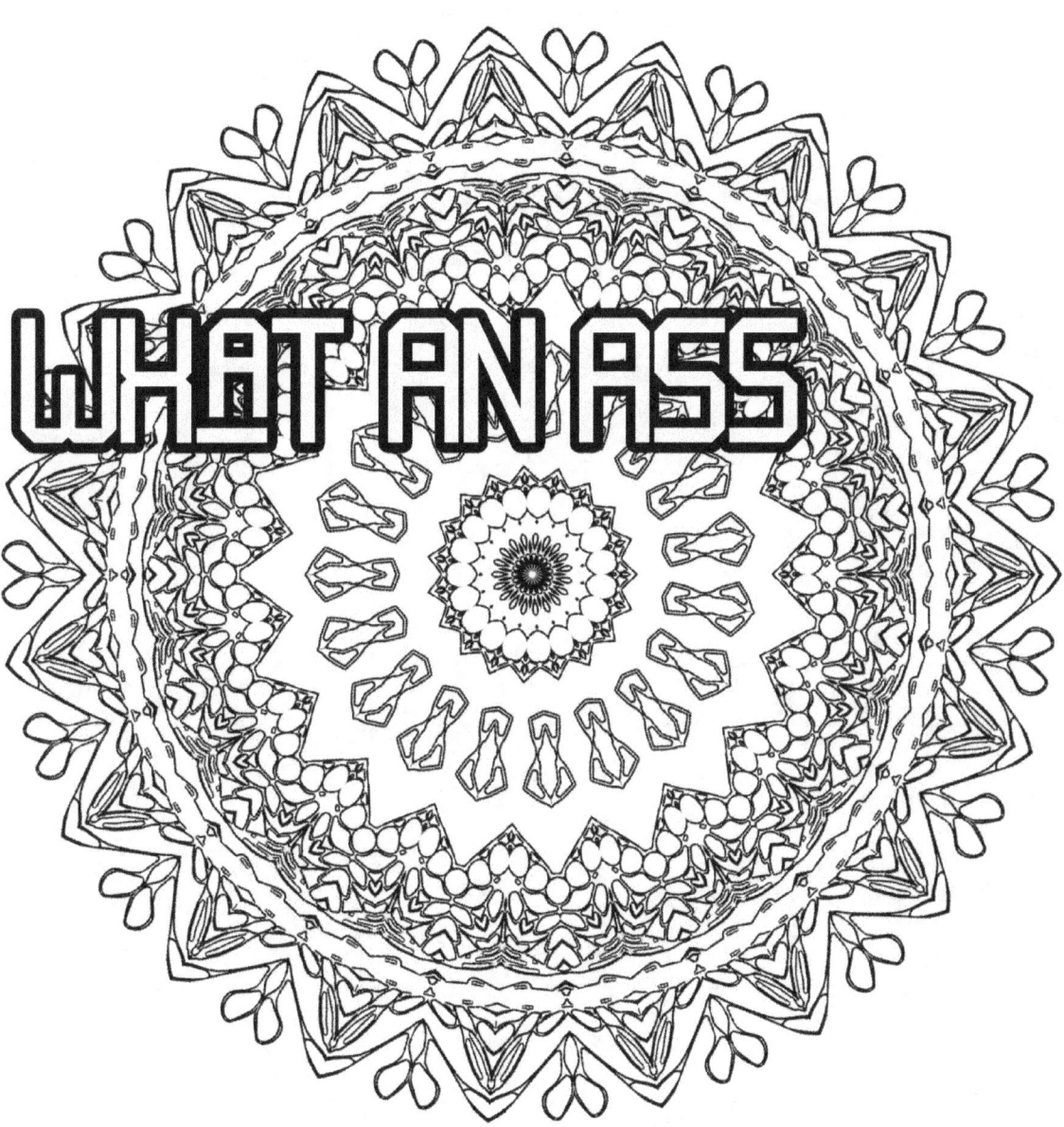

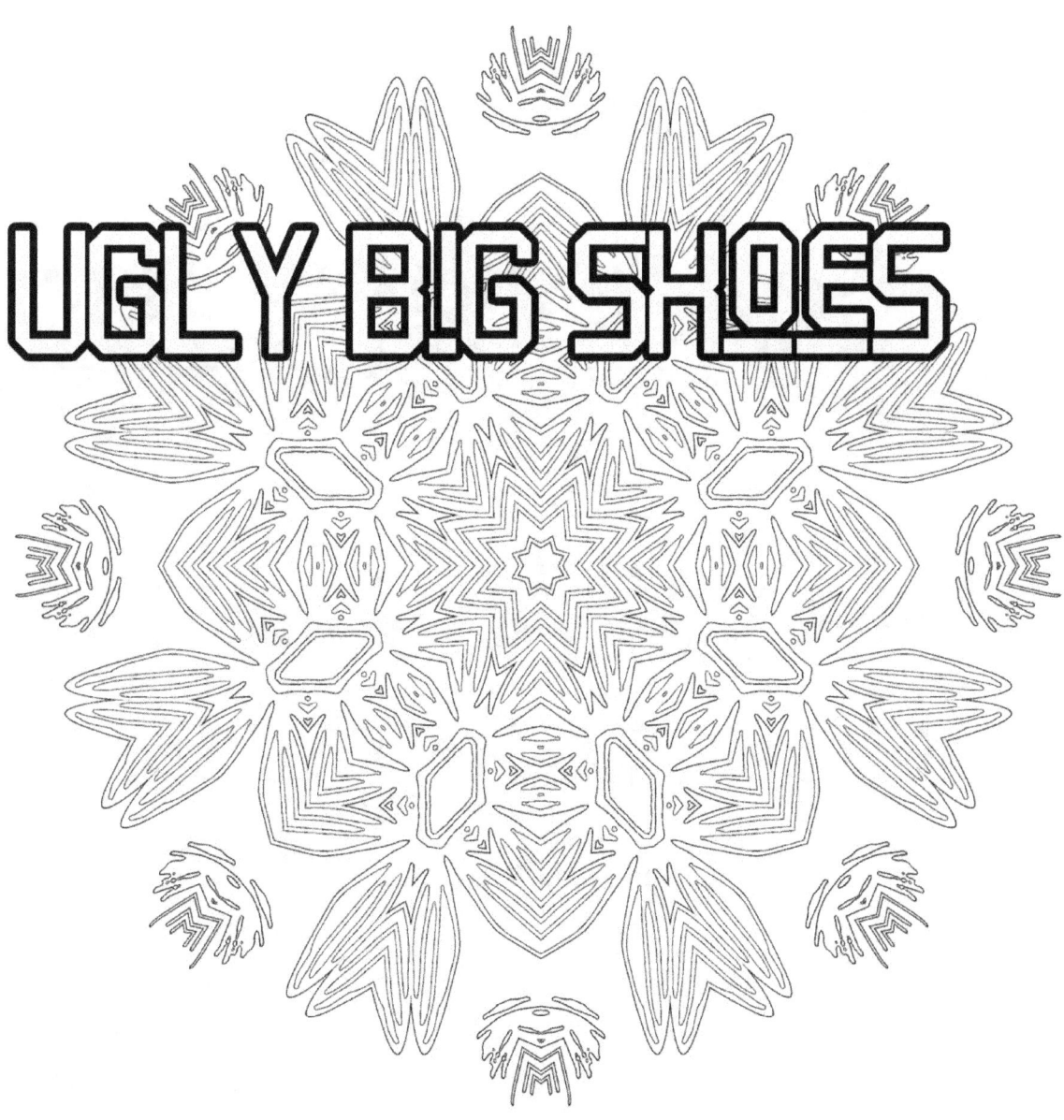

UGLY BIG SHOES

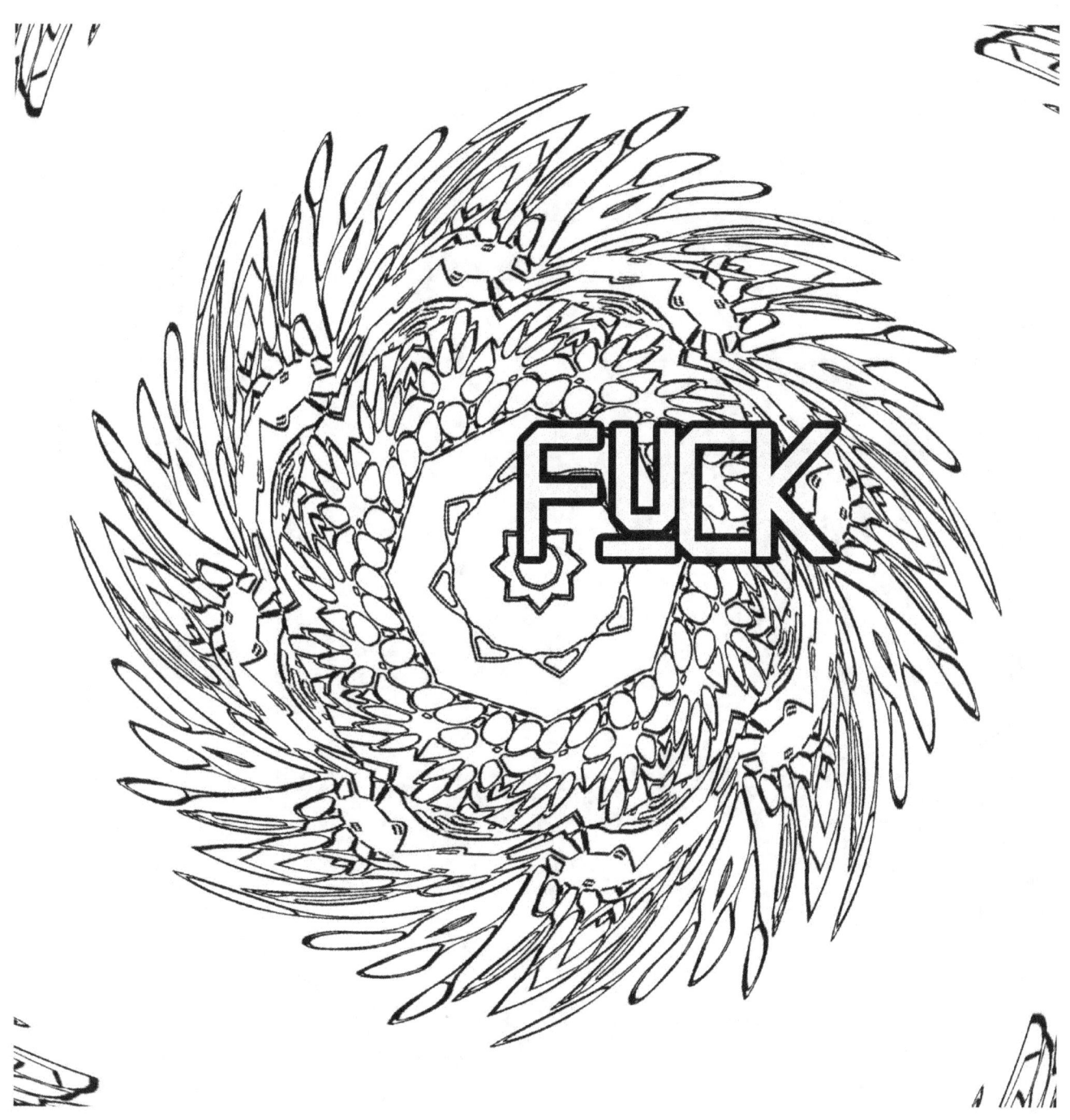

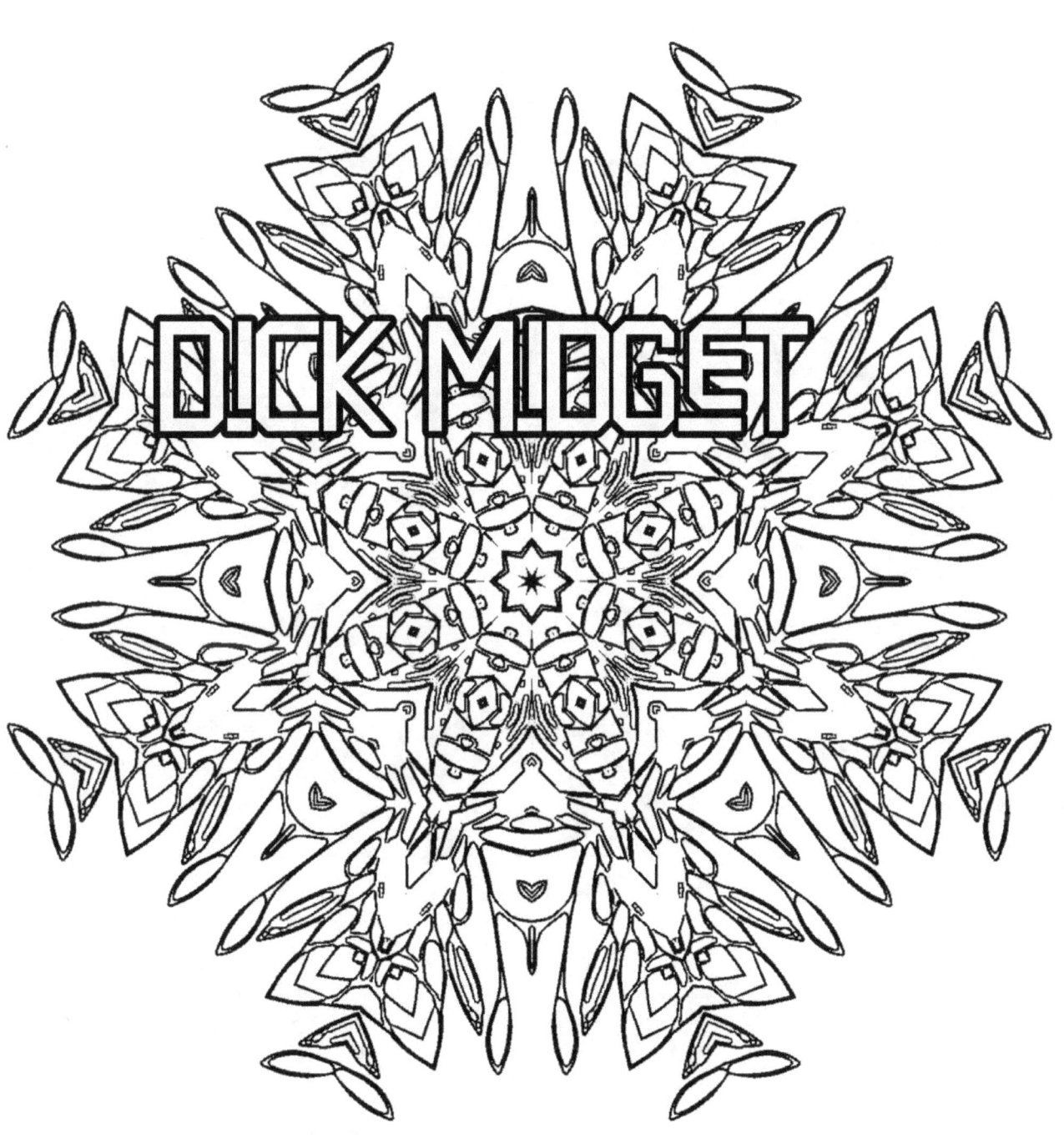

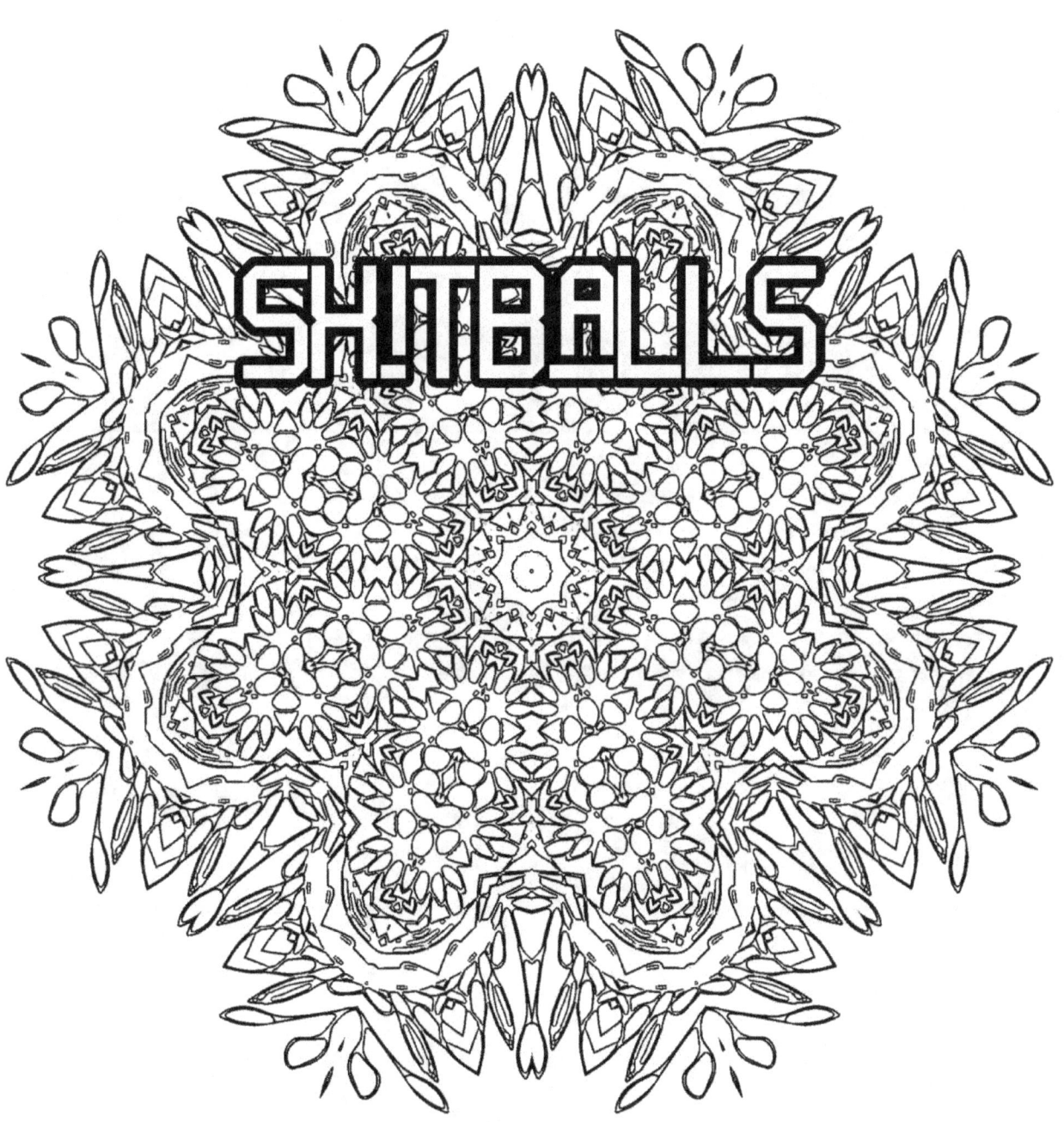

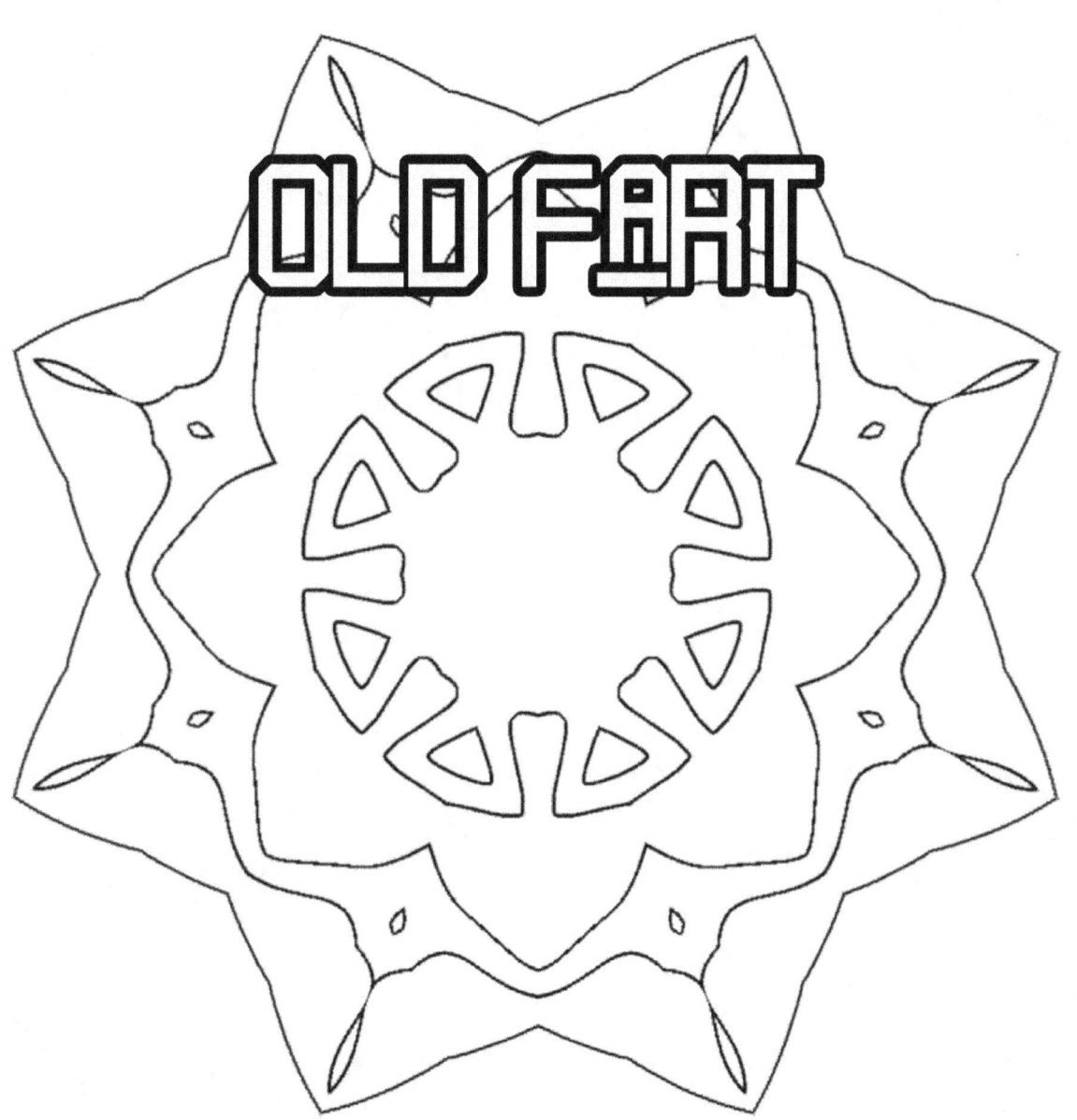

OLD FART

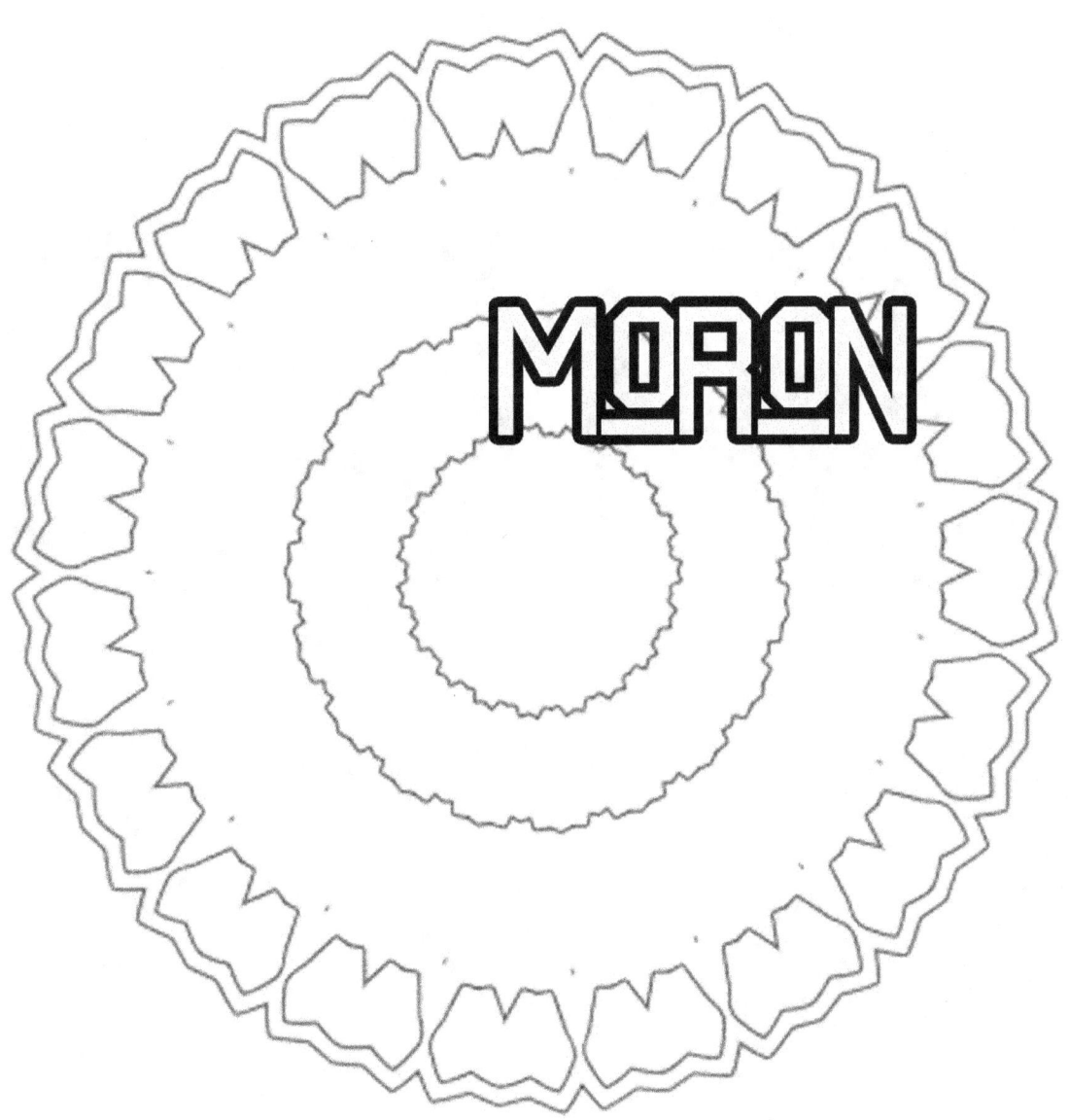

MORON

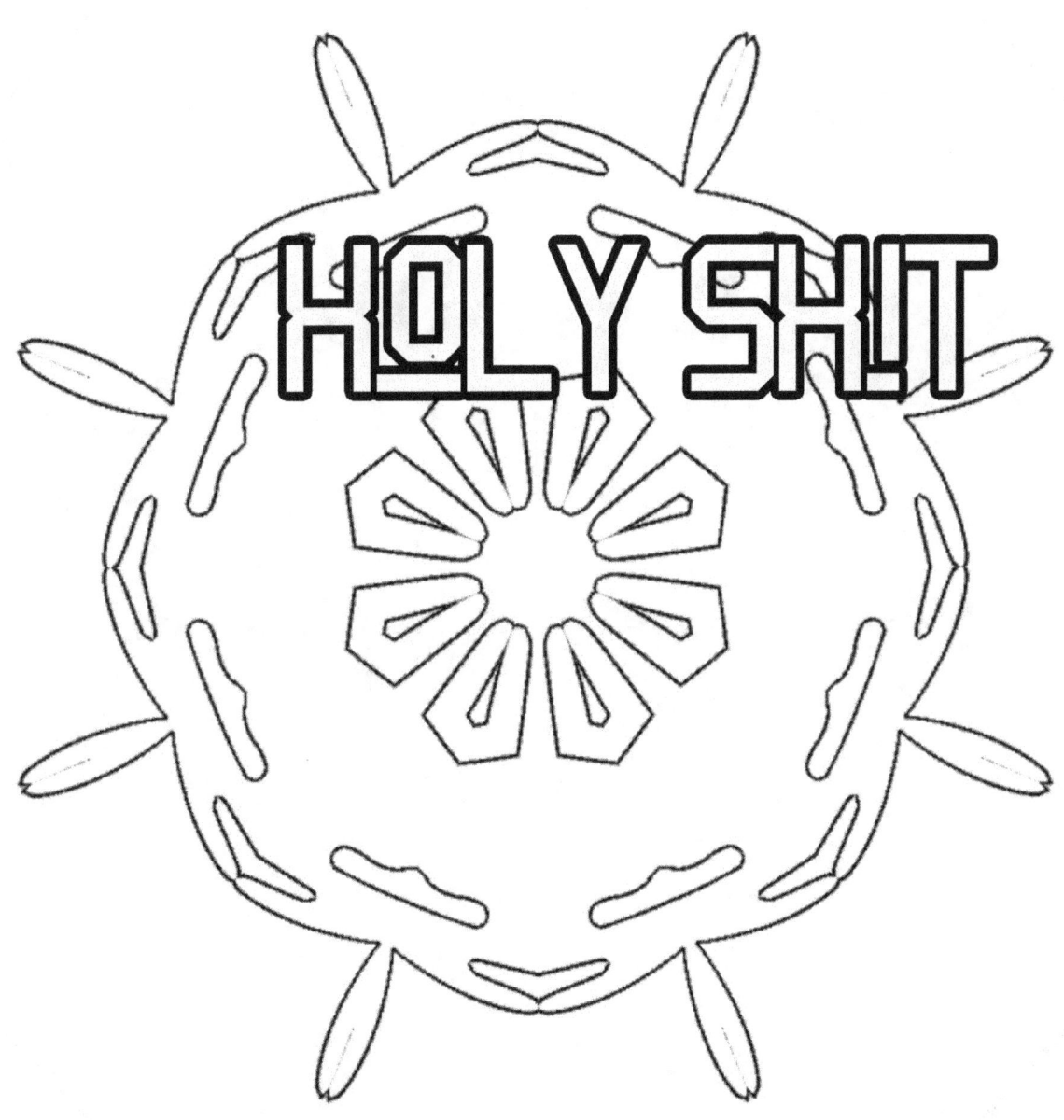

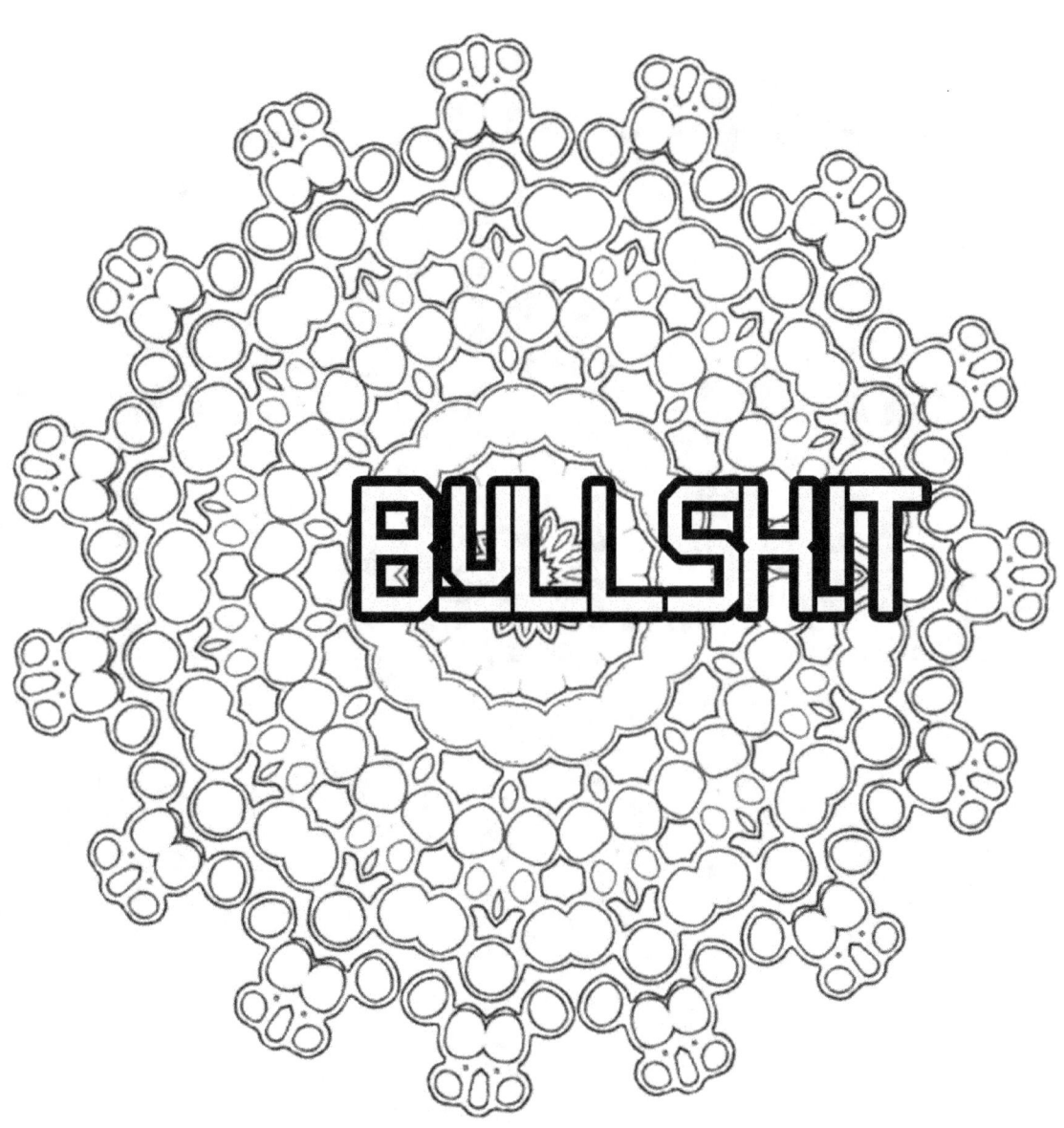

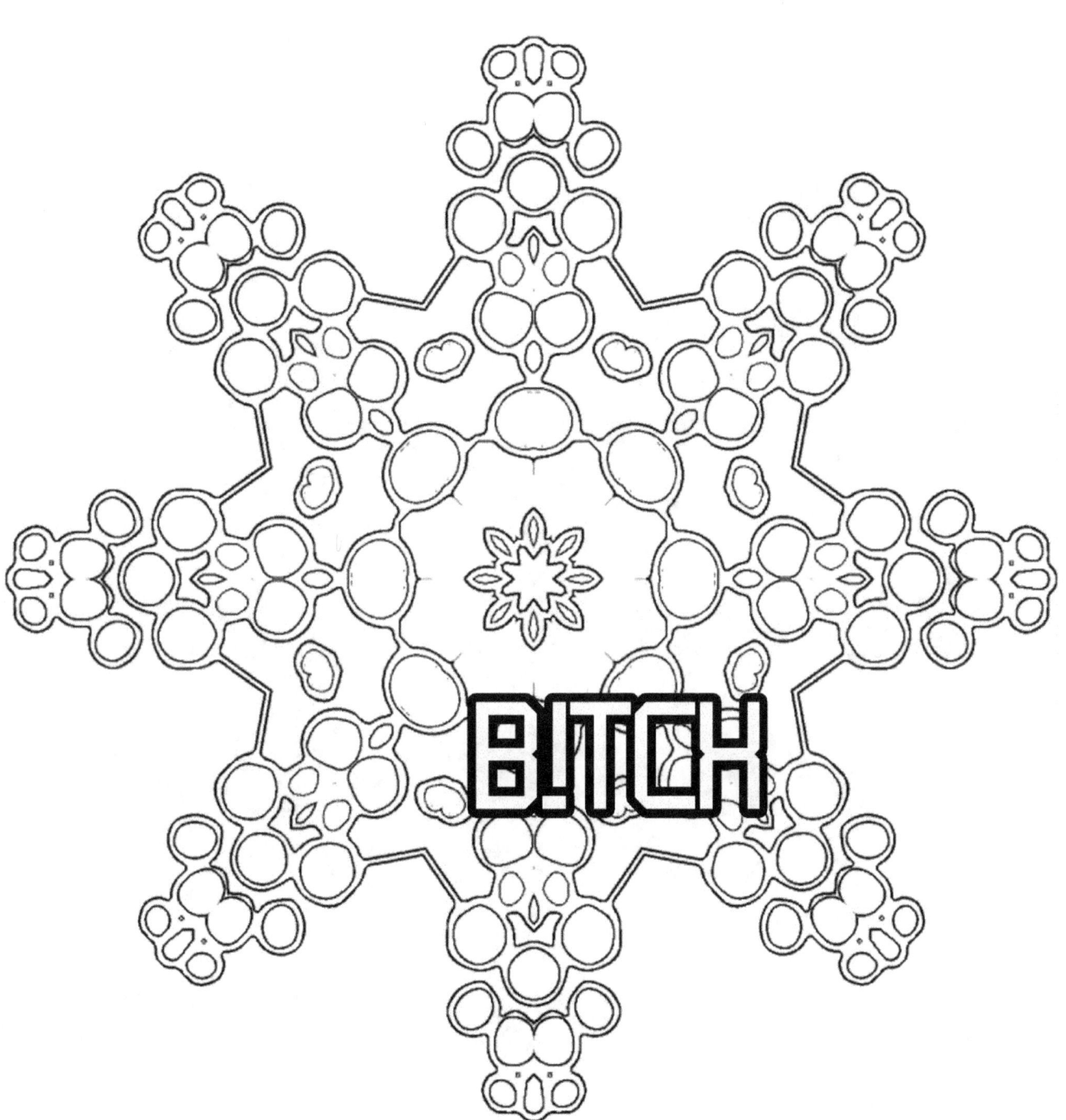

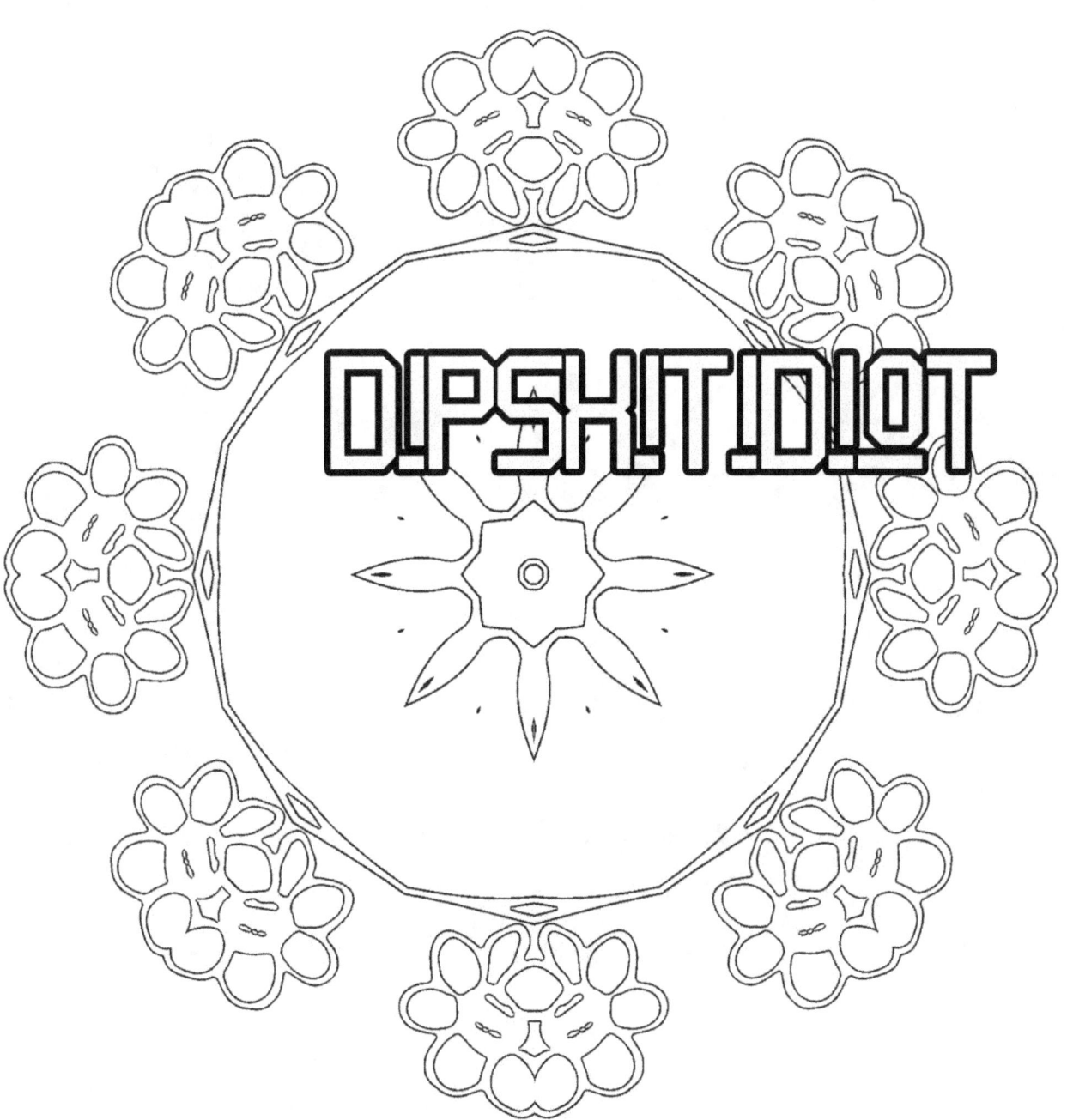

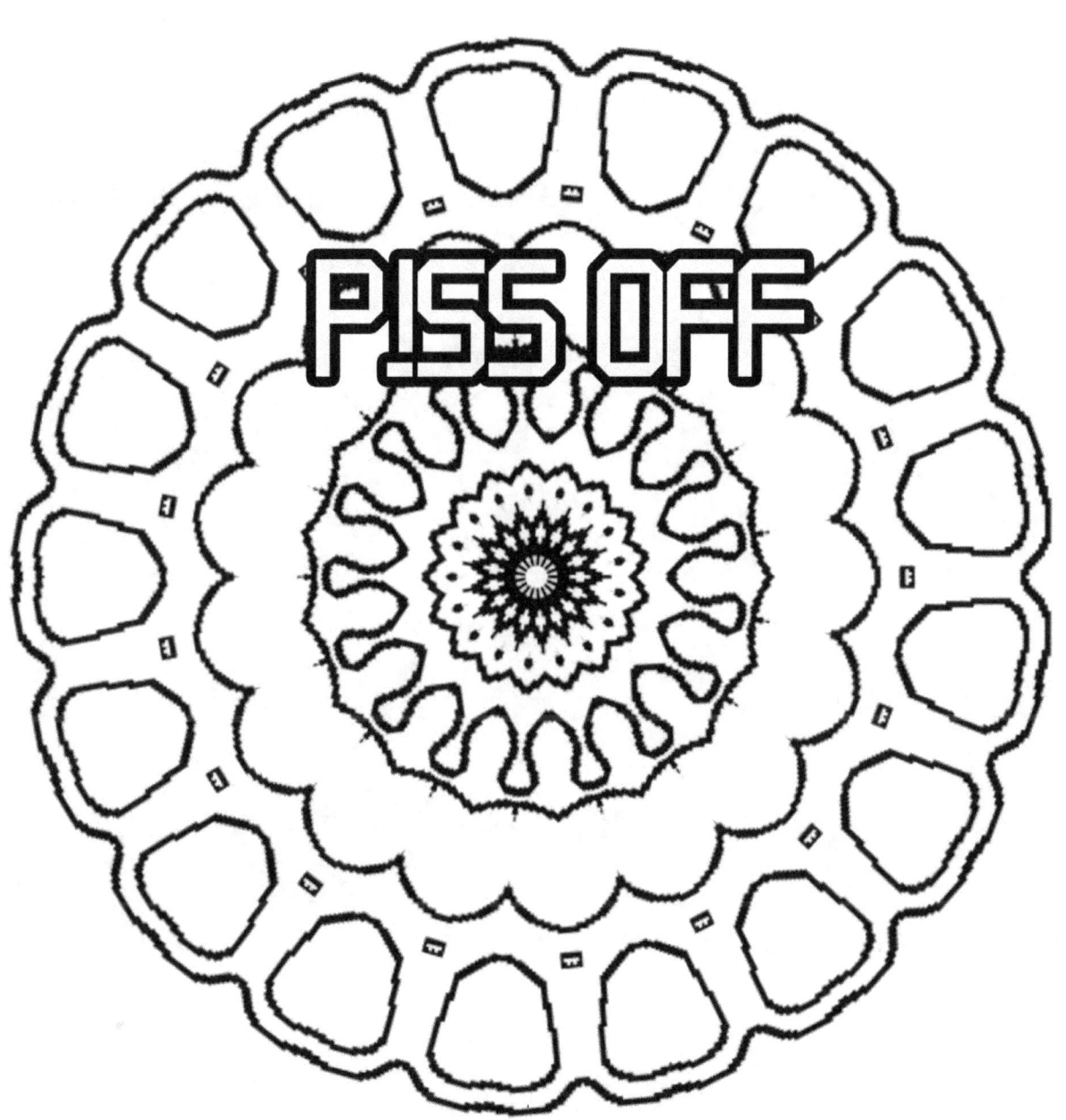

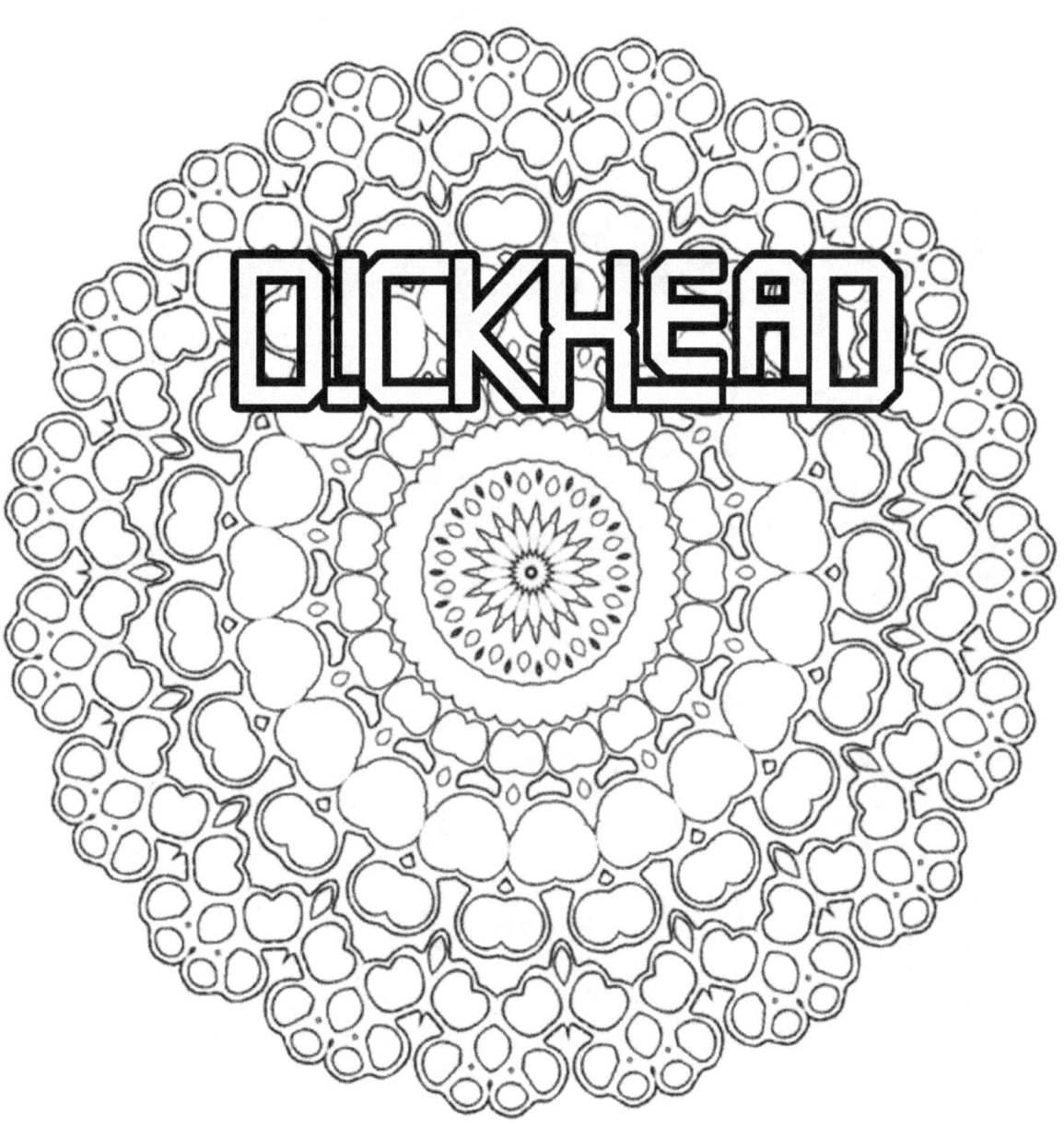

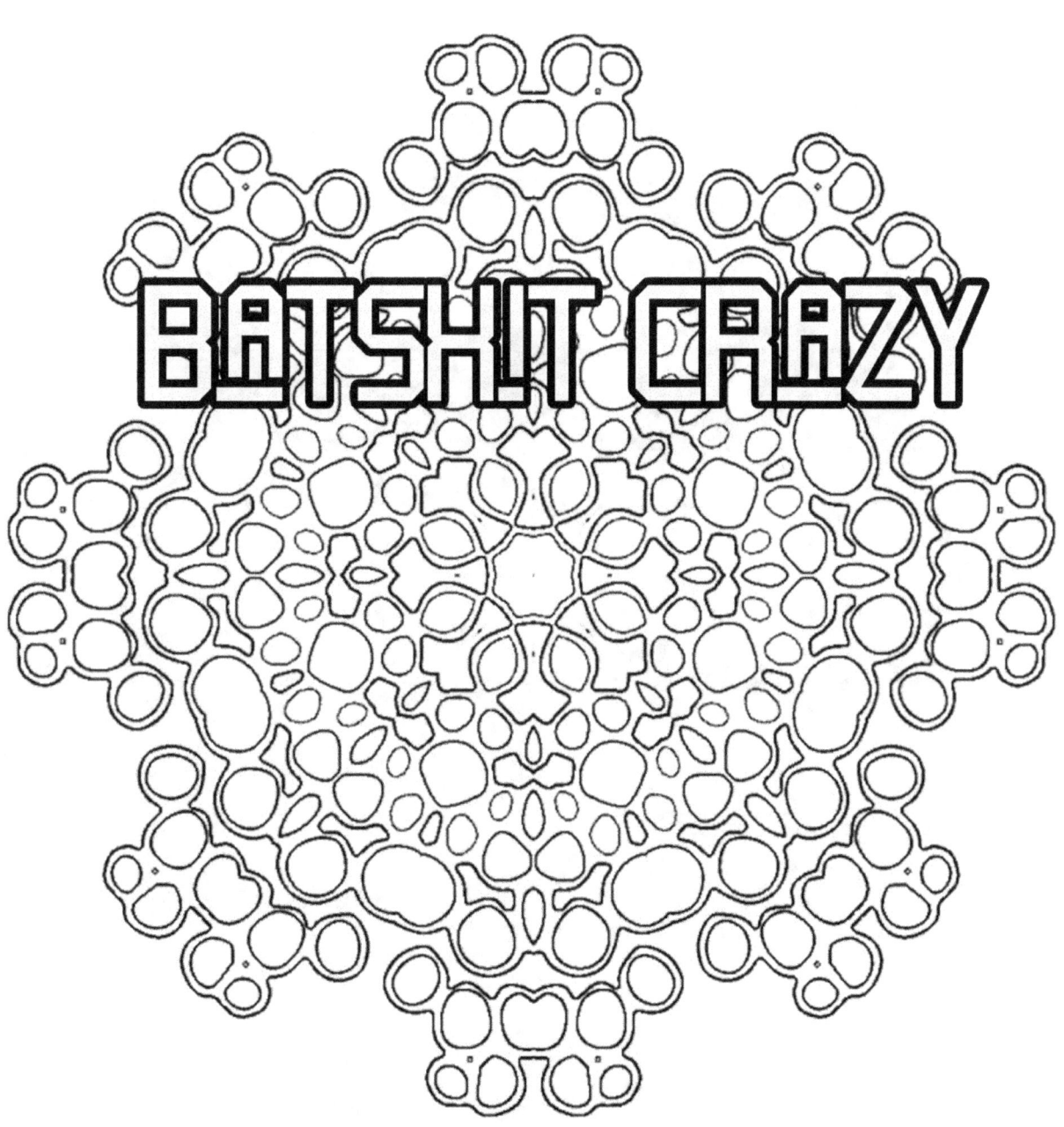

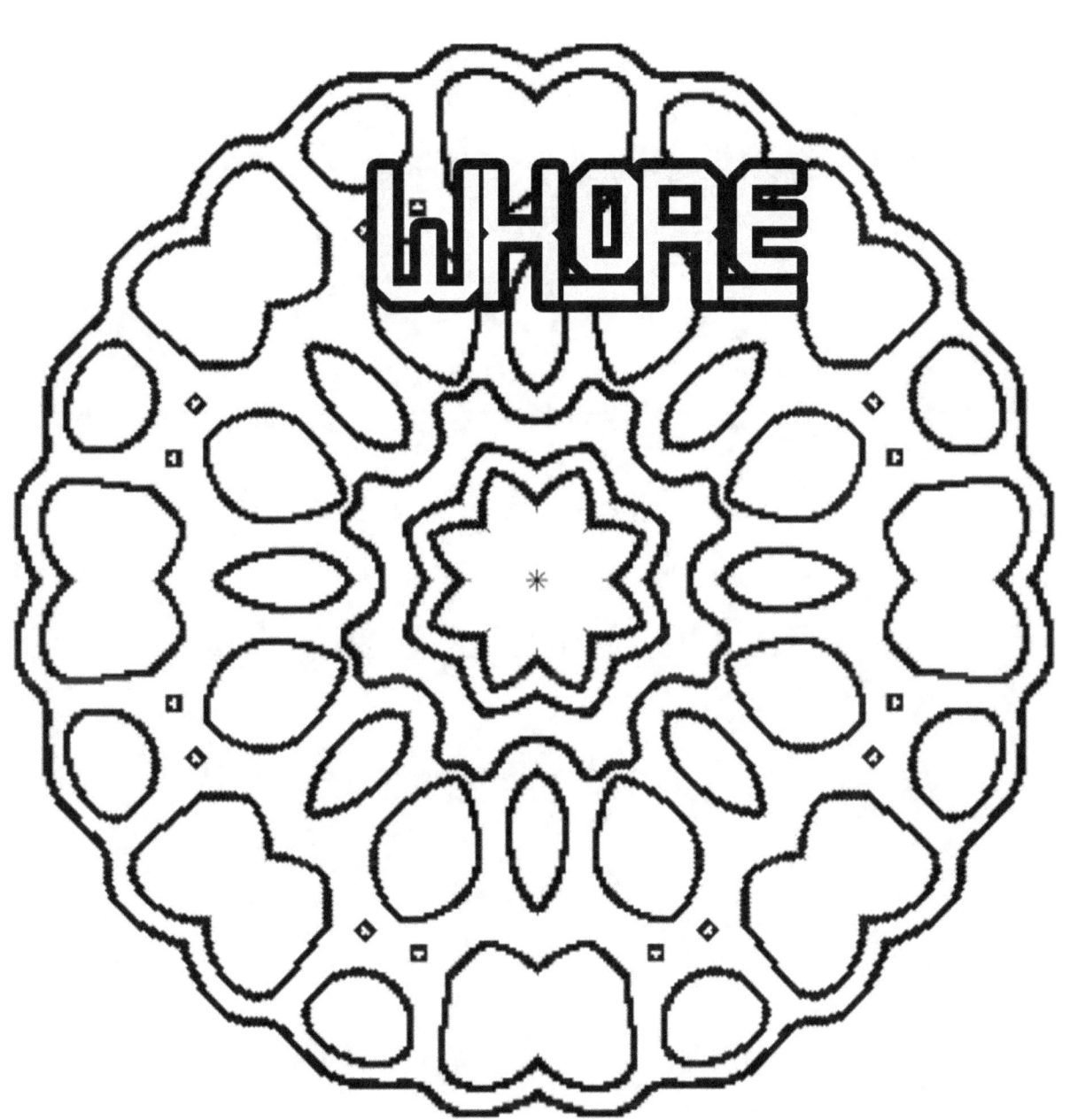

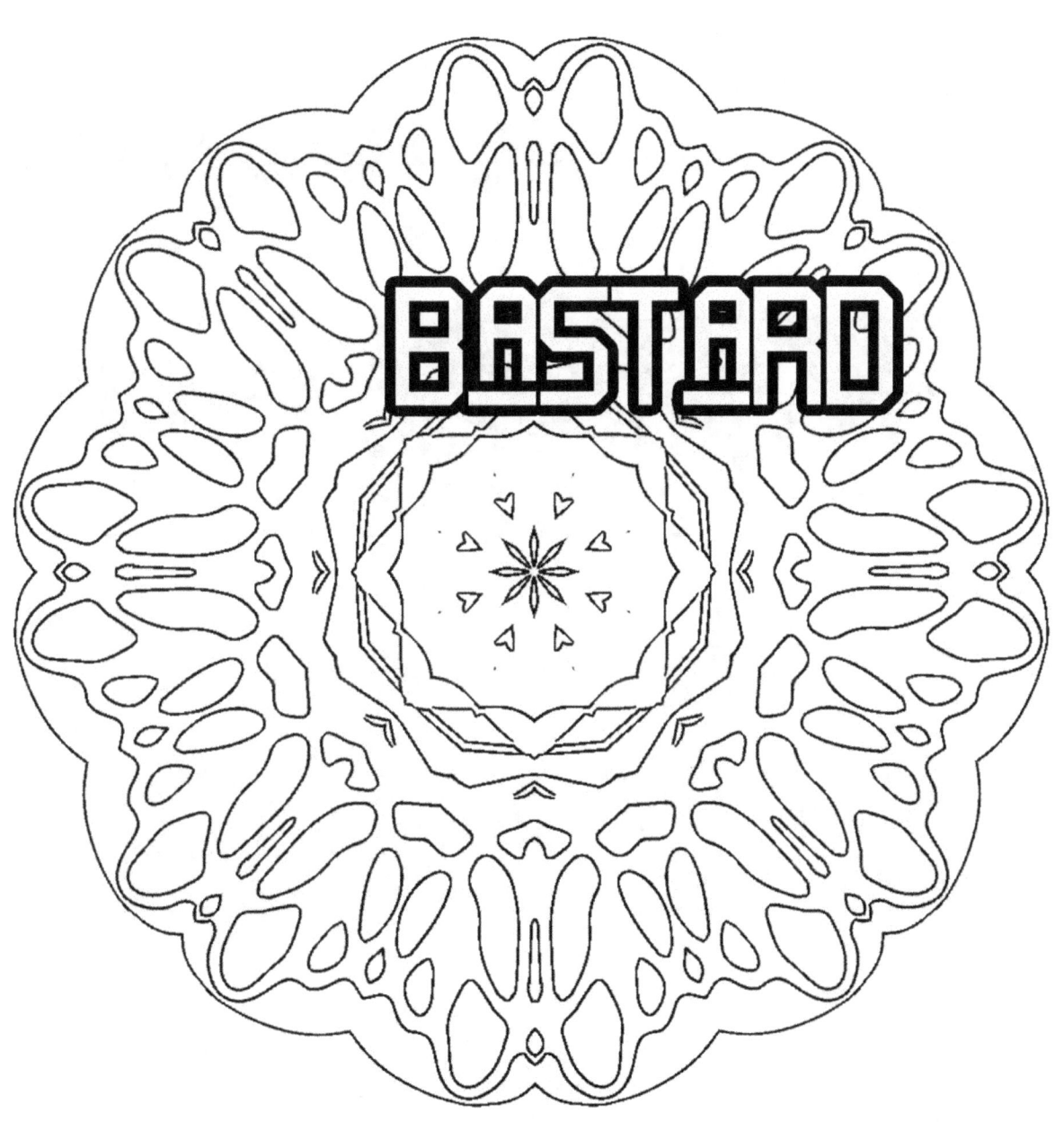

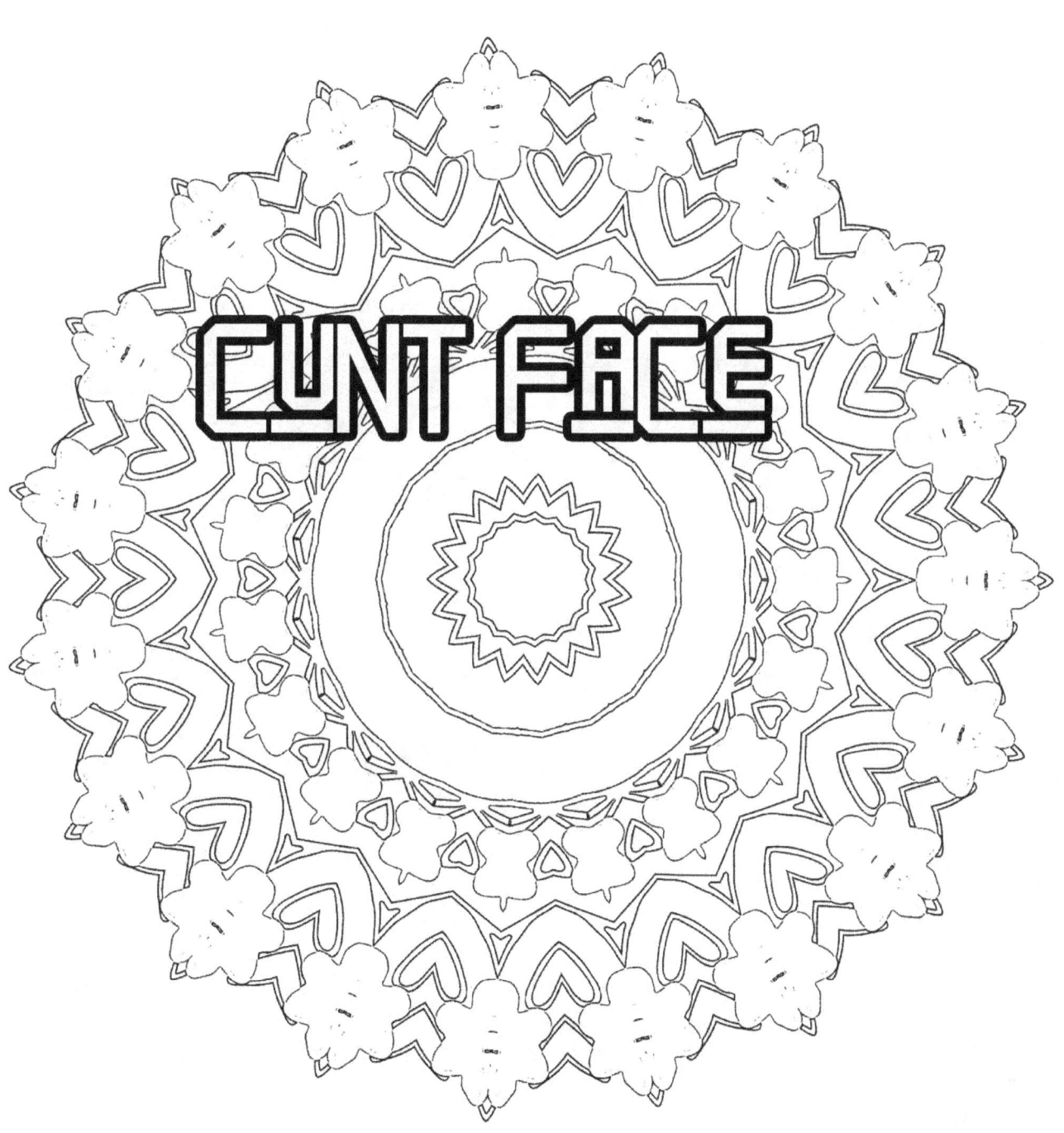

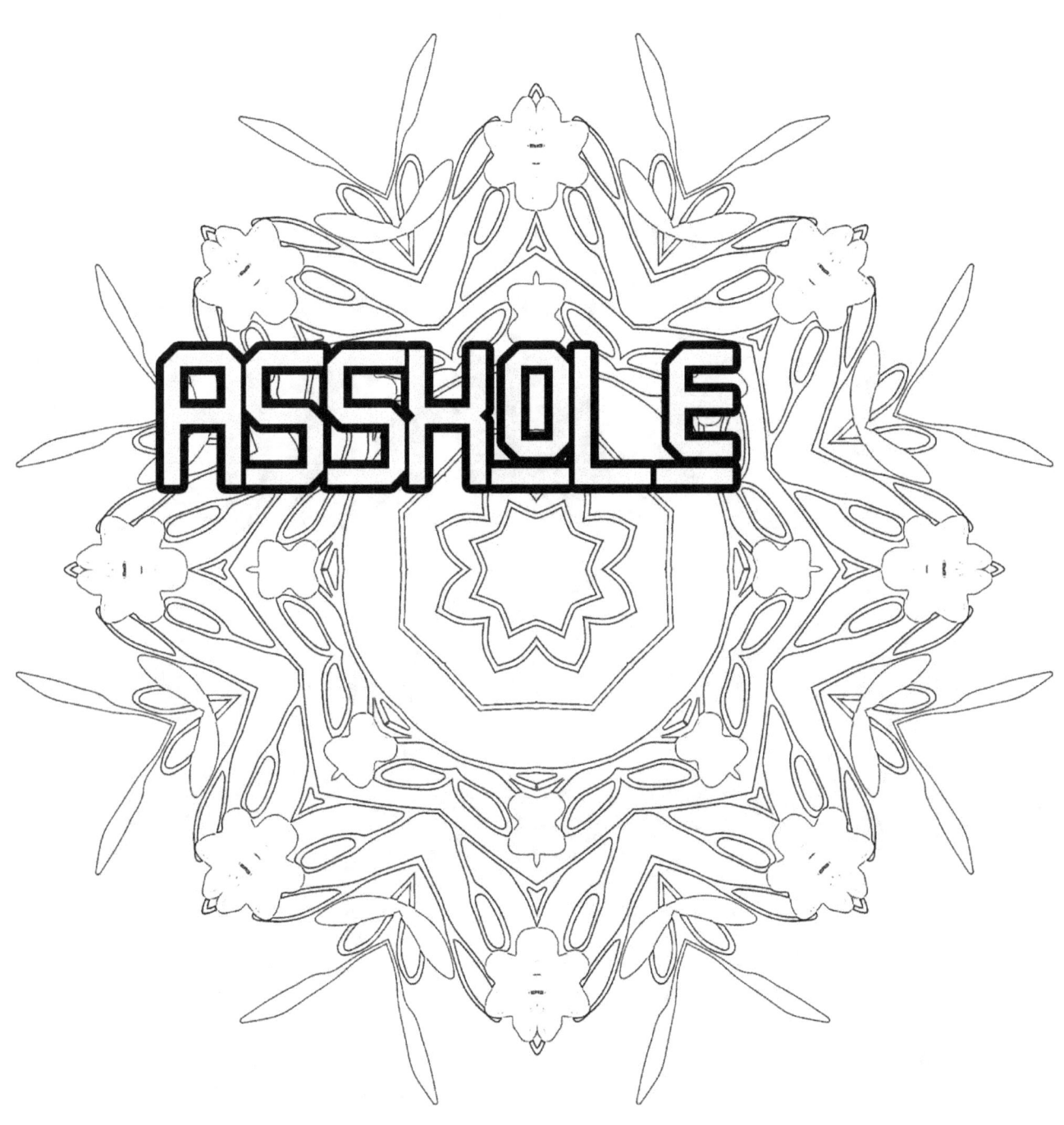

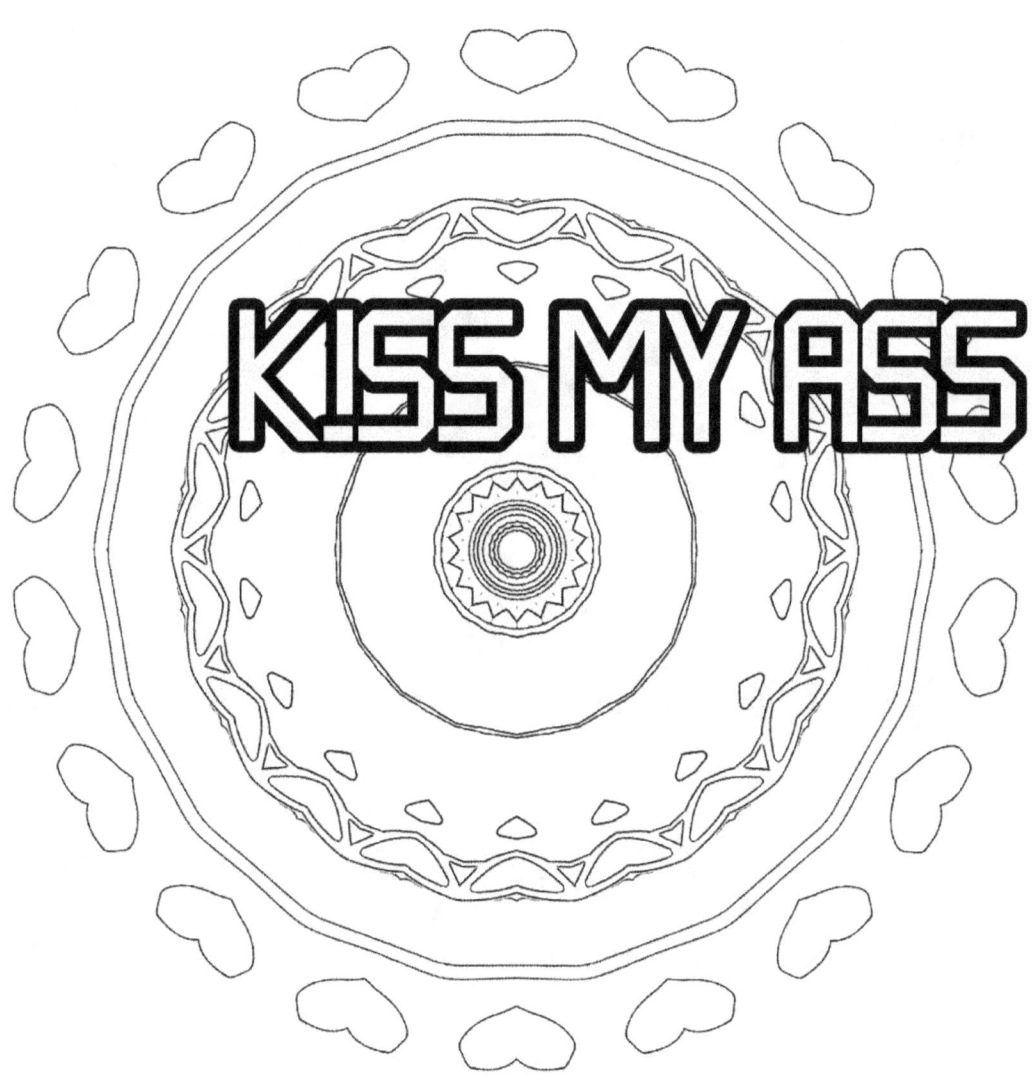

KISS MY ASS

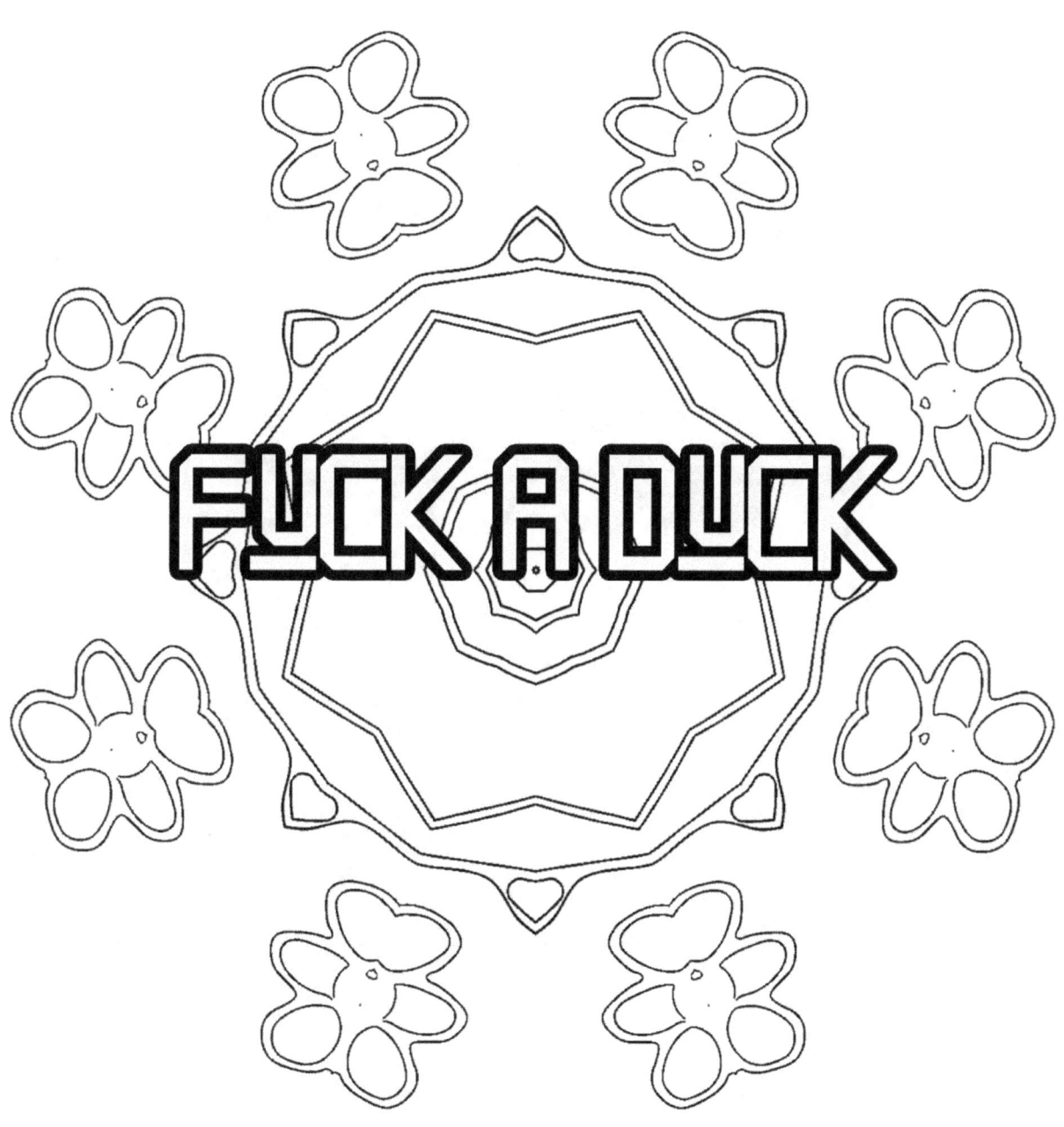

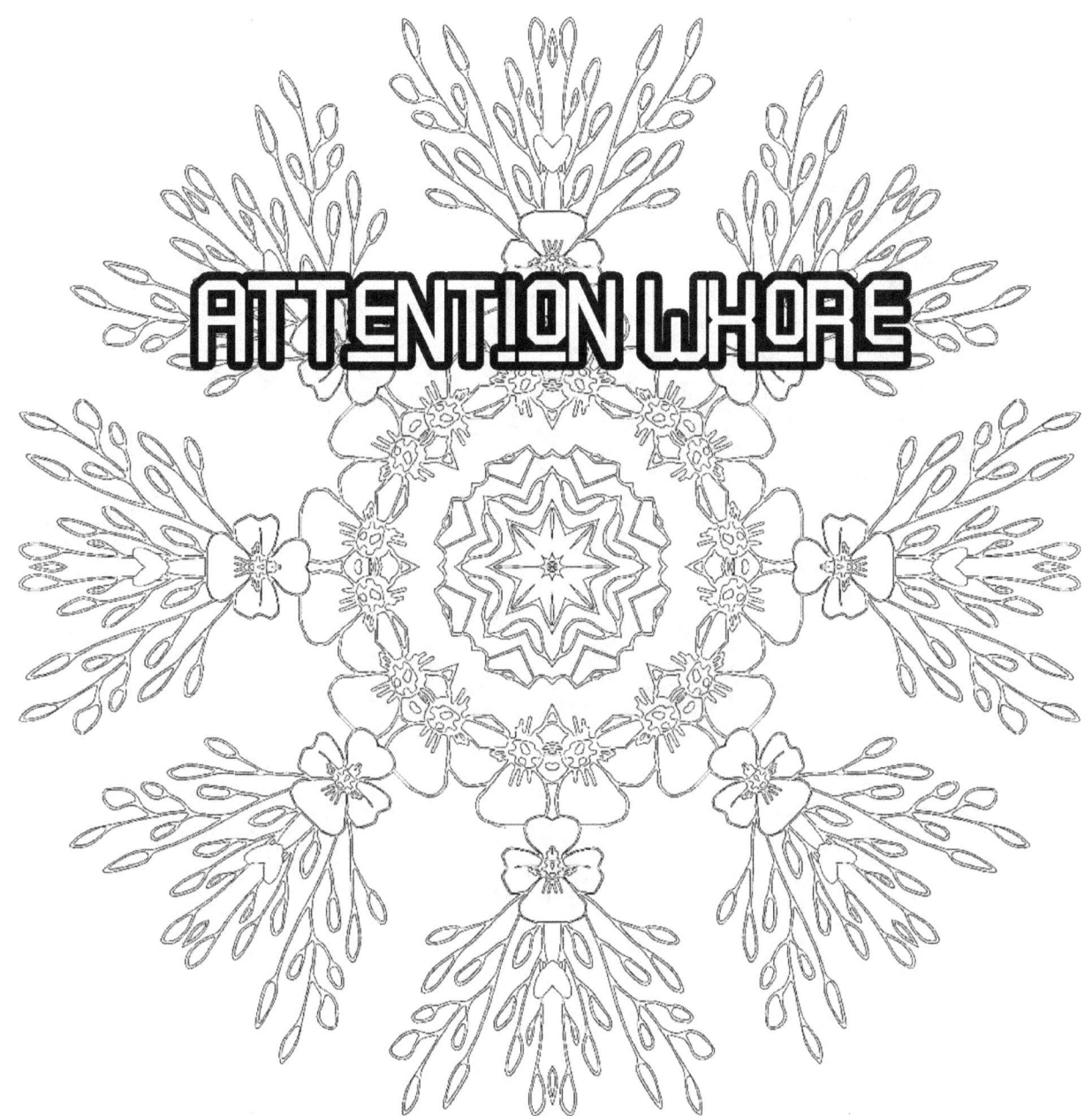

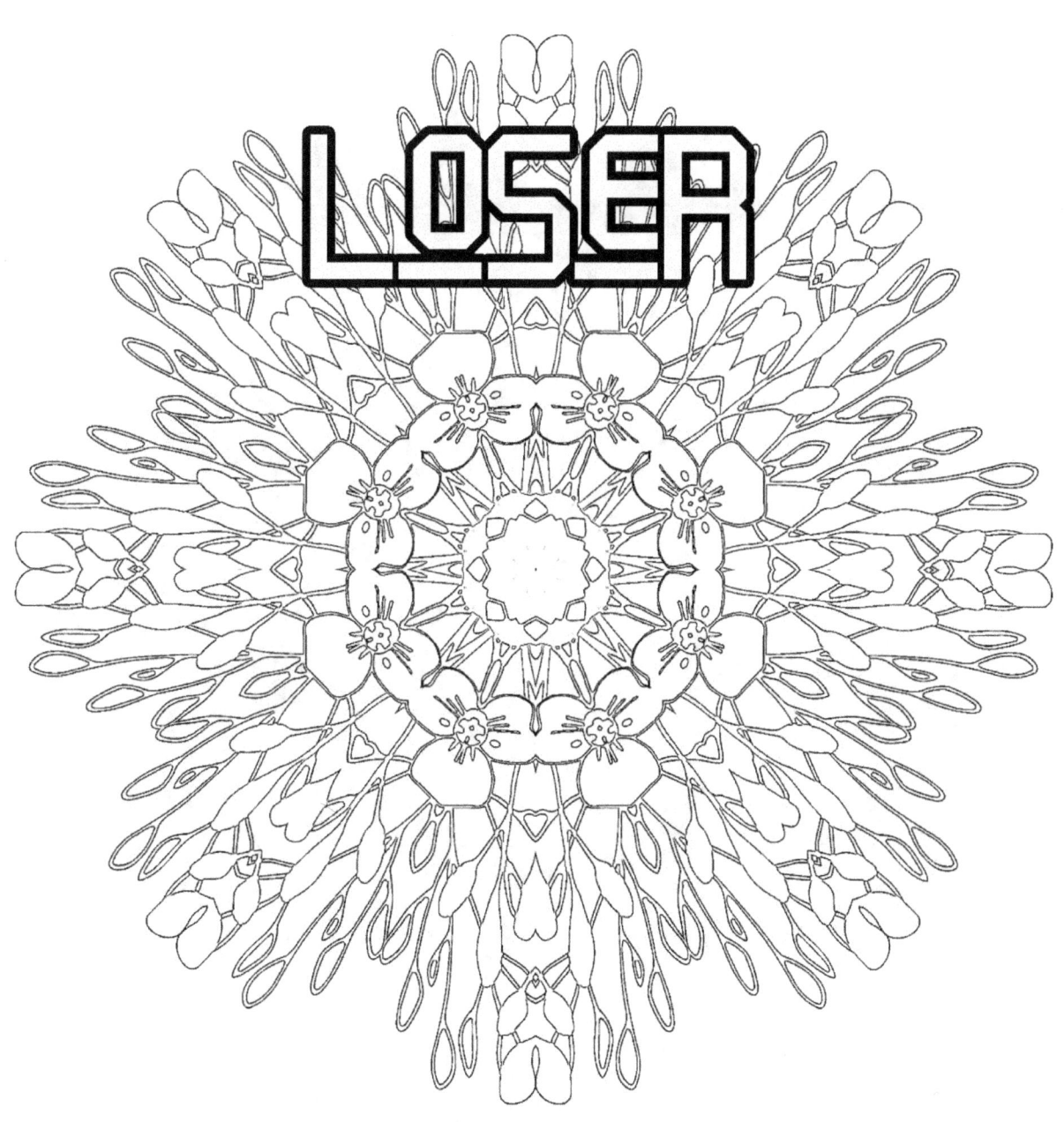

www.ingramcontent.com/pod-product-compliance
Lightning Source LLC
Chambersburg PA
CBHW081751170526
45167CB00009B/3994